As One

Like Christ and the Church

As One

Like Christ and the Church

REGINALD C. HOLDER

REDEMPTION PRESS

© 2017 by Reginald Holder. All rights reserved.

Published by Redemption Press, PO Box 427, Enumclaw, WA 98022

Toll Free (844) 2REDEEM (273-3336)

Redemption Press is honored to present this title in partnership with the author. The views expressed or implied in this work are those of the author. Redemption Press provides our imprint seal representing design excellence, creative content, and high quality production.

No part of this publication may be reproduced, stored in a retrieval system, or transmitted in any way by any means—electronic, mechanical, photocopy, recording, or otherwise—without the prior permission of the copyright holder, except as provided by USA copyright law.

All Scripture quotations, unless otherwise indicated, are taken from the Holy Bible, King James Version, © 1979, 1980, 1982 by Thomas Nelson, Inc., Publishers. Used by permission.

ISBN: 978-1-68314-560-8 (Paperback)

Library of Congress Catalog Card Number: 2017960685

Table of Contents

Chapter 1: Learning from Home 13
Chapter 2: The Great Command 21
Chapter 3: The Condition of the Church 27
Chapter 4: The First Marriage 35
Chapter 5: Help Arrives 43
Chapter 6: Adam Was There 47
Chapter 7: Do You Know Her? 53
Chapter 8: The 100 Percenter 61
Chapter 9: My Story 67
Chapter 10: The Percenter Continued 73
Chapter 11: A Good Man – The Provider 79
Chapter 12: A Good Man – The Priest 91
Chapter 13: A Good Man – The Prophet 103
Chapter 14: To Nourish and to Cherish 109
Chapter 15: The Big Payoff 117

Dedication

I HAVE MANY people to thank for pushing me and supporting in the birthing of this work, but only after I first thank my Father God. Thank you, Father, for giving me so many do-overs after all my blunders.

There is my pastor who we call "The Great Illustrator and Teacher," Bishop Horace E. Hockett, and First Lady Elder Kiwanis Hockett. You have loved me and allowed me to grow with liberty and grace.

Additionally, to all those who were willing to be interviewed on the spot and give your insight to this work. To Karynthia Phillips for all the advice, patience, and guidance.

To my three children who continue to give me exceedingly more joy than this daddy deserves. My parents, Richard and Nola Holder, who assured that all your children were introduced to Christ and the scriptures at an early age.

Then there is the love and encouragement from my beautiful wife, Dr. Greta Manning, without whose push I may have quit on this process.

My forever girlfriend, Thank You.

Foreword

IN ECCLESIASTES 1:10 Solomon asked, "Is there anything of which one can say, look! This is something new…?" This question is often asked about books on marriage. We may believe we know or have heard it all, but be advised, to keep our relationship strong, regular maintenance is required.

On any given Sunday, you can look out over a congregation of well-dressed couples praising God and giving the impression of a stable and substantial marriage. However, a large majority of these couples are struggling to maintain their well-dressed facades.

Like most pastors, I have spent many hours in pre-marital, marital, and divorce counseling. I have also found that Proverbs 11:14 rings true. "Where no counsel is, the people fall: but in the multitude of counsellors there is safety."

This book is a relevant and timely resource. It gives sound practical counsel for those desiring to strengthen or repair their marriage.

I have witnessed Reggie's journey through a difficult season of his life. Each subject addressed in this book is a testimonial to Reggie's devotion to family and the application of God's principles. My adoration and trust in him as a progressive servant of God has only increased.

Yes, this is another book on marriage, but it is written from a layman's perspective. It is written by one who sought and followed sound biblical counsel and reaped the blessings of God.

We all know that marriage is a complex, yet rewarding status if properly entered and prayerfully maintained. On the pages of this book you will find invaluable lessons that will help fortify your marriage as you live out God's will for your life.

—Bishop Horace E. Hockett

Preface

MEN HAVE HEARD for years that they are to love their wives. The issue with this advice is they are never told how this is to be accomplished. Many methods have been tried with varying successes and failures. What I missed in my life was the lack of real love being displayed in front of me. I never saw a flesh-and-blood example of how a man was supposed to love his wife.

My questions were, "How do I put real love for my wife into practice, each and every day? What are simple ways to love my wife?" Then there is also the biblical command to deal with that tells me to "love [my] wife as Christ also loved the church." Is there anyone who is doing this?

As One: *Like Christ and the Church*

In undertaking these questions, I spent lots of time in prayer to God and in conversation with others seeking out answers. As I traveled, I'd walk up to total strangers and pose the question, "How does a man love his wife the way Christ loves the church?" I asked men and women. I asked young and old. I asked church people and non-church people. Some of the answers I received are included at the beginning of each of the following chapters.

The remainder of this book explores the different roles men play in marriage. It's important for men to know their wives well in order to be able to love her sufficiently, so another question this book deals with is, "Just how well do you know your wife?" In order to work through all these questions, the reader will find practical daily tasks to follow throughout the book. By the turn of the final page, each man will find that he is encouraged to present his wife unto himself just as Christ will present His bride to Himself. Husbands and wives truly can live "as one."

"Be the role model of love in the home."
—William Myers

CHAPTER 1

Learning from Home

I WAS BORN into a family that was every bit the prototypical American family of the 1960s and 1970s. Dad was the primary breadwinner. Being a carpenter by trade, Dad worked hard. He not only worked as a carpenter, but he always had that extra job; you know, the one he went to after his regular work that we called a "side hustle." Mom was 80 percent homemaker in our house and 20 percent part-time employee outside the home.

Our story is similar to many others we've known or heard about, as our economic status varied between lower middle class and just plain "po." Mom checked the grades while Dad checked the conduct, and with five siblings interacting, there was always something going on. Dad would often say, "I have my word and my name. Don't mess with that."

We spent lots of time with our extended family and stayed involved in activities such as scouting, sports, plays, and of course, church. Mom and Dad both served in various areas in the church and this meant we children were visible and active as well. We were expected to be really good and to behave without succumbing to the normal temptations of almost everyone else in the world.

No such luck for me because as I came into my teen years, I started noticing the different equipment females were blessed with (and that I liked what I saw). I also realized that no one talked about how to properly relate to the opposite sex. A real talk was not the tenor of the day. So how did we learn? It just happened.

Sex and expressions of physical tenderness were just not talked about around the church, in the neighborhood, or at home, and public affection or outward demonstrations of love and tenderness were non-existent. It was said that outward demonstrations of love by men indicated weakness. The men around us would never have wanted to look weak, so most of the time, there wasn't any affection toward their wives to observe.

I remember my mom once saying to my dad that he hadn't said he loved her in a long time, much less shown her his feelings toward her. The look on his face trying to figure out what she wanted from him was priceless. He looked as if he wanted to ask, "Really? You really mean this?" He was stunned by Mom's statements. And why shouldn't he have been? In his day, if a man worked hard, came home with the money, applied discipline to the children, and supplied protection for the wife, he was a good man and his actions were enough to say, "I love you."

With this being the standard measure in my dad's mind, he knew he was doing good. As a husband, he thought himself to be at least a seven and a half to eight on a scale of ten, but Mom wanted more and she persisted in making it plain by spelling it out.

Her questions came fast and furious. "When have we gone on a date? What about dinner for just the two of us? When have you bought me flowers or a card that was not on my birthday, on Mother's Day, or from the kids?"

I was now looking at a man I'd never seen before. My dad was a man who was perplexed and stunned. He had no answers, even though he was always resourceful in other ways. If we needed it – food, clothing, shelter – he found a way to get us what we needed. If something was broken, he found a way or a friend to fix it.

But this sensitive stuff Mom was asking for, these matters of the heart, this reaching deeper inside than he ever had reached before, had crippled him. He was at a loss concerning how to meet the requests of the wife he loved.

Finally, he said back to her, "Are you saying you're not happy?"

Mom just turned and left the room with a final statement to my dad, saying, "You just don't get it."

A couple of days later, after enduring very little interaction or conversation with Mom, Dad came home with flowers. Yes, flowers! He walked over to her, and with all the tenderness he could muster he said, "Okay, take 'um." Now remember, this happened in the early

Learning from Home

1970s. When I tell you of Mom's shock, she was floored! Yes! She absolutely loved it. Her response was complete with tears and nerves as if it were her first date.

I am telling you all of this to give you a view of the beginnings of my life's perspectives on male/female interactions. Music, movies, television, and the older guys on the street were outside influences that also gave me a somewhat limited, yet also expanded points of view on relationships outside of my home environment.

As I continued my own journey to maturity and manhood, I began to leave the God I knew as a child to embark on a real, much deeper relationship with Him. I wanted and needed to know more, both about God and about relationships. When I finished high school and began college, my relationship with God had been more or less dependent on the prayers of my mom and the discipline of my dad. It was time for me to grow in my personal knowledge of God and my experience of walking with Him. I began to read the scriptures. I didn't do a word study or take a specific course; I just read the Word. Starting with the New Testament, I read it from start to finish and started over again. After about four times through, I began to add the Psalms and Proverbs. It was at this point that the Holy Spirit began to slow my pace down, as I would stop and ponder a passage or a word.

One day, when I was married with a family of my own, Ephesians Chapter 5, verse 25 "leaped off the page" at me. It said, "Husbands, love your wives even as Christ loved the Church!" My wife and I were mostly happy and content, but I was also working with a limited, outdated, or even broken model of what a loving husband should look like. My wife at the time had not been raised with her father in the home, which made it difficult for her to express her needs to me; therefore, we mostly operated by trial and error.

Years passed by, and after a lot of ups and downs, my wife and I eventually divorced, but even then, I could never shake Ephesians 5:25. "Husbands, love your wives even as Christ loved the Church!" The words kept running through my head. I couldn't get past this portion of the verse.

And thus, my journey of inquiry and discovery began concerning being a godly husband. So, come with me as we go on this journey together learning how to love our wives "as Christ loved."

"Treat her right. Just treat her right!"

—Pastor Myett

CHAPTER 2

The Great Command

THE STRUGGLE TO find the perfect balance of the many aspects of the relationship for a husband and wife is a never-ending process. Each person in every couple longs for his or her own space, independence, importance, and purpose in this of all relationships: marriage. Because of the struggles faced around these and other issues, marriages can become strained, stressed, and tested. When things are good, both parties work to find the necessary balance, but if couples are not careful, things can easily get offtrack.

This world we live in offers many challenges and obstacles to maintaining the delicate balance of all aspects of every relationship. We experience many things that can (and often do) come against our marital union including pride, selfishness, careers, family, finances, coworkers, other people, and an innumerable array of other situations.

To say the least, marriage takes work. This union is so important to God that He compares it to the relationship of Christ and the Church. What is the relationship between Christ and the Church? In a nutshell, the Church is considered His bride and He loves her. So, what's a man to do? Every husband is tasked with loving his wife as Christ loves the Church.

I can hear your thoughts. *What? Love her as Christ loved the Church? As Christ loved the Church? Really? How? What is the true meaning of such a statement?*

These are great (but unnecessary) things to consider, for in scripture, this is not a question, but a command from God. The entire verse of Ephesians 5:25 states, "Husbands, love your wives, even as Christ loved the Church, and gave Himself for it." I don't hear a question, do you? This command is not optional. There is no wiggle room or latitude. This Bible passage is clear and definite. Husbands are to love their wives just as Christ loved the Church. Wow!

We tend to focus on the latter part of this passage ("and gave Himself for it") and zoom in on the great sacrifice of our Savoir. Many men do not give it a second thought to sacrifice for their families, not allowing anything or anyone to harm or threaten their wives and kids. Some proclaim with all the bravado they can muster, and pledge to fight to the death for their loved ones. While this can make for great commentary, moving sermons, and great macho statements of manhood, these proclamations don't speak much to the realities of day-to-day living.

As men, we can easily become acclimated to the idea of sacrifice and work as we accomplish the many tasks, duties, and responsibilities in life. Many of us become workaholics, thinking our sacrifices of time in providing for those we love will prevent and solve our problems. But is this the love God was speaking of in this verse?

Furthermore, marriage is not a task. A task is something to be assigned, completed, or solved. Marriage is much more, and our wives certainly aren't problems to be solved. Men who have the outlook that marriage and women are tasks find their marriages shallow and troubling to say the least.

You see, marriage is a covenant not to be entered into lightly or in ignorance, but sadly many men and women do just that. They enter what is to be a lifelong endeavor without consideration for the commitment marriage calls for, and most alarmingly, they say their "I Dos" without any knowledge of all that marriage entails. Therefore, many couples end their marriages before they've even begun the journey.

Before Christ gave Himself for the Church, He loved her. Yes, Christ loved and still loves His bride. The Bible tells us that He eventually died for her, but He loved her first.

Why did He love her? How did He love her, and furthermore, how does He love her today?

Even more than that, how can a man love any woman to the same degree or the same standard as that of Christ? Is it out of reach for the average man to love his wife the same way Christ loved the Church?

Women are longing for the love of a godly man, but most men feel they are incapable of such love.

Where are the men who will seek the will of God for their wives and children? We seem to find men who are willing to die for their wives and families, but where are the men who are willing to live for them? Yes, live for them, and love them – love them as Christ loved the Church.

As Christ loved the Church! Wow!

Let's look more deeply into this mystery and seek God's wisdom on the matter.

> "Unconditional love is what she needs. Hang in there with her through it all, for better or worse."
> —Deacon Freddie Hunt

CHAPTER 3

The Condition of the Church

WE MUST KEEP in mind that both men and women are included when the Bible talks about "the Church." When we consider just how Christ loves the Church, we must also consider the extent to which He loves each of us.

After the Fall of Adam, all of humanity needed a Savior. All of humanity was separated from God; we were all lost. Women were not any more lost than men. Both women and men need the Savior. Even though some men think women needed and still need more work, we were all lost and in need of the Savior. "For all have sinned and come short of the glory of God" (Romans 3:23).

And yet, there are men in the new millennium who still think that women are somehow below them in the pecking order of authority, if there is such a thing. They still believe that women were placed on earth only to serve them and meet their desires.

Men must come to grips with the fact that their own logic and reasoning are but a shadow of the purpose of God. When left to contemplate the cycle of life, the origin of man, and our purpose in this world, we are but blind men who stumble in the dark. Oh yes, we've made advances and discoveries in this world. We have come up with witty inventions, new toys, and technologies that make our lives more comfortable and convenient; nevertheless, none of this ingenuity would have come forth without the omniscient God ordering it. Left to ourselves, we are most miserable. We can find nothing that will satisfy the deep craving for fulfillment that exists within each of us until we receive God's salvation and come into the greatest relationship we could experience – the relationship of oneness with God through Christ.

The Condition of the Church

Mankind is separated from God and in such a miserable condition thanks to Adam and Eve. Yes, the great Fall of Man that happened in the Garden of Eden ripped all humanity from its unobstructed relationship with God by introducing sin into the mix. And there was no hierarchy in the Fall. Fallen is fallen. When mankind fell, all of mankind fell. Neither side was in any way more a sinner than the other. In this Western society, we try to rank and rationalize sins with some reasoning that the woman's sin somehow caused the man to sin. God has no such ranking system, and when Adam tried to use this defense, it was quickly dismissed. The good news is that reconciliation was needed by all and is available to all.

The Fall of Adam and Eve brought a separation between God and man. God's judgment fell upon man. The Father was never pleased with mankind in this fallen state, nor was He content to be out of relationship with His most precious creation. God would establish His covenant with His chosen servants (Moses, Noah, and Abraham, to name a few) and nation (Israel),

As One: *Like Christ and the Church*

despite how mankind continued to commit grievous sins against Him.

Over the centuries, mankind has tried many things in hopes of making its way back to God, but what lacked in these efforts was the reality that the efforts were not done God's way. Man still trusted himself way too much, thinking he could figure out in his own mind and reasoning how to bring about reconciliation with God. Man did not realize that only the Creator Himself could provide the way back into relationship with Him.

God provided the ultimate sacrifice and the way of reconciliation of man to Himself in His Son, Jesus Christ. Christ was sent to bring salvation to a lost world. This includes men and women. We all needed and received the same level of reconciliation. Jesus died on a cross, was laid in the tomb of Joseph of Arimathea, arose from the dead, and ascended to the right hand of the Father for us all.

So, even though Christ was sent for the Church and He loved the Church, His focus was not the will of the Church. His focus was never what the Church

The Condition of the Church

wanted. His focus was always the will of the Father. It was the will of the Father for Christ to live, die, and rise again to reconcile mankind to Himself.

The will of the Father being done was the sole motivation of Jesus. He never sought the desire of the Church or that of the people. Not even His disciples fully understood this. Remember, they (like most of the Jewish world) were looking for a political leader to come and overthrow the Roman government. Even after months of being in His company, they wanted to erect a monument to Him on the mount of transfiguration. Whenever He spoke of his impending death and resurrection, they initially didn't understand Him (which led to Peter's misguided attempt to correct/rebuke Jesus).

As the family of God, the Church is to have the same focus and attitude as Jesus did, to do all things that please the Father. We, the Church, are the benefactors of Christ's obedience. Because He is in the Father and the Father is in Him, Jesus has the same love for the Church that He has for the Father.

The misunderstanding comes when the Body of Christ, the Church, or the individual believer does not truly comprehend the love God has for us. The Bible says, "For God so loved the world that He gave His only begotten Son" (John 3:16). Can you stop for a moment and try to comprehend a God who "so loved" you? This love was the sole motivation for Him to send His Son.

We must keep our hearts fixed on the love God has for us if we are to even think of truly loving a woman. While focusing on the shortcomings and missteps she has in her womanhood, we cannot be blind to the same missteps and shortcomings we encounter on our journeys as men. Oh yes, we are a flawed band of brothers, "but God commended his love toward us, in that, while we were yet sinners, Christ died for us" (Romans 5:8).

Therefore, as we ponder this command to love our wives as Christ loved the Church, we must keep in mind our own plight and road to redemption. There is no room for comparisons or accusations, no finger pointing or blame. The position of the man and the woman toward God must be one of thanksgiving. We must live in a state of thankfulness to the Lord for being the way out of bondage and the way back into relationship with God the Father.

> "I need love, leadership, and guidance. He must be my confidant and counselor."
>
> —Amy Westly

CHAPTER 4

The First Marriage

AS WITH ANY great command or commandment in the Bible, to understand it we should start at the beginning, the book of Genesis. Here we find recorded more than the creation of the heavens and the earth, we also find God's order being established. In the creation, certain limitations were set, allowances were made, permissions were given, and boundaries were established. It was during the creation week when light and darkness were separated. The stars were set in place and told how brightly and how long to shine. The waters below and above the firmament were separated.

The sun, moon, Earth, and other planets were established. The seas were told to recede and uncover the land of the earth, but also to go only so far on the shore and not an inch farther, for the boundaries of the tide were set.

And man was created on the sixth day.

God gave man dominion, commands, orders to follow, limits, responsibilities, and an occupation. These responsibilities were God-directed, God-breathed, and God-spoken. In other words, these were God's executive orders. As such, all the words God said constituted His will for man and were not mere suggestions.

Oh, and about that occupation: yes, man did have work before he had a woman. Remember, this is God's order, but this is not about just having a job. The first man was performing the duties that he was created to do. Adam's "work" – a calling, if you will – was the occupation he was designed and gifted for by God.

God first established a certain character in the man before the woman was ever introduced to him. The later command "to love [his wife] as Christ loved the Church" takes much more than just being gainfully employed. Taking a spouse is an undertaking of responsibility and self-denial.

Adam was placed in the Garden of Eden (Genesis 2:8). Why was he placed there? He was placed there to commune with God and to "dress and keep" (cultivate) the garden (Genesis 2:15).

Dressing the Garden

When the first man was set in that blissful place, it was not intended for him to just hang out there as if it were simply a place of observation. He didn't only have a paradise to observe, enjoy, and live in. He also had a paradise to watch over. Yes, there is always responsibility, even in paradise. So, what was involved in the "dressing" process?

To dress means:
1) to labor, do work ;
2) to work for another, serve another by labor;
3) to serve (as subjects) to be worked, be tilled (of land);
4) to serve (God);
5) to be enticed to serve (as with Levitical service); to make oneself a servant to be worked; and

6) to compel to labor or work, cause to labor, or cause to serve.

"To dress" also carries the same meaning as the duties of a worshiper, as these tasks and responsibilities are performed as a labor of love, and are carried out in the context of relationship.

This man had real work to do, but dressing this garden didn't mean he had to plow the fields or plant seed, for God caused all the plants to reproduce after their own kind. He didn't have to water the garden because God caused a mist to go up from the earth and water all creation (Genesis 2:6); nevertheless, this man was under the authority of God to oversee God's territory.

Can you imagine the joy of flowers blooming and the original songs the birds were singing as Adam, the jewel of all creation, moved throughout the garden? Each day was filled with discovery in worship to the God of the entire universe. Adam was serving God in the earth. His posture was one of obedience and worship directed to the Father.

In light of the call and love that the Father had for Adam, he was placed in the utopian environment with the mandate to work. This was not a "J.O.B." as we know work. Jobs, labor, and sweating came because of the Fall of man (Genesis 3:19). The dressing process was one of relationship with God. This was a process of Adam discovering his best self.

Can you imagine walking hand-in-hand with God as you discover each day more and more about God and about yourself? The more Adam communed with God, the more he discovered about himself. Adam could soak up the essence of God in a face-to-face relationship. Just imagine walking and talking, shoulder-to-shoulder with God as He taught you and showed you Himself.

What an exuberant time of self-discovery Adam must have had when he realized that he was like the Father – made in His image. As such, Adam was participating in the continuing creation process with God. After all, it was Adam who named all the animals, and whatever he called the animals, those names remain today.

What an awesome existence was Adam and God's daily fellowship before the Fall! Talk about authority, power, companionship, and responsibility! Just as Adam named the animals, perhaps he also named the plants and trees except for the Tree of Life and the Tree of Knowledge of Good and Evil because God specifically introduced Adam to these trees. The rest of creation also needed to be identified, including trees, bushes, flowers, and the like. Who better to complete this larger naming task than the man created, gifted, and entrusted by God with the responsibility to take care of it all?

Think of how great of a life we all could experience even now if we would take the time to walk and talk with God just as Adam did.

What makes our walk more spectacular and fulfilling is having Jesus as our Advocate and Intercessor. He has taken our place and paid the price for sin; therefore, even when we fall our relationship is never at risk.

Keeping the Garden

Adam was also charged to "keep the Garden."
To keep means:
1) have charge of;
2) guard, keep watch, save life;
3) to watch for;
4) to observe, celebrate;
5) to preserve, protect.

Adam was the watchman, the protector, the observer, and the one to celebrate all the works of God's hand from the vantage point of worship, responsibility, and experience.

Added to the blessing of being the caretaker of the Garden, this is also where Adam resides. He may have even done some landscaping from time to time to enhance the beauty of his home.

Adam had been given the rank of overseer with orders to preserve and protect the garden. He is placed there as God's servant and guard, but let us also notice the military/law enforcement image that is presented.

Remember that a huge part of "keeping" the garden was also celebrating and saving life. Before the Fall, Adam was on point to serve and protect, and God was pleased.

> "It's all about me. The love he shows is that our love is all about me."
>
> —Camillia Redish

CHAPTER 5

Help Arrives

WHILE ADAM WAS going about his business of taking care of the responsibilities of the Garden of Eden, it came to God's attention that all the creatures on the earth had a mate except for this man, Adam.

God said, "It is not good for man to be alone; therefore, I will make for him a helpmate suitable for him" (Genesis 2:18). Here she is!

When Eve arrived, Adam was excited. The Bible says he saw her and proclaimed "…bone of my bone and flesh of my flesh: she shall be called Woman" (Genesis 2:23). Eve was stunning to look upon; a supermodel if ever there was one since she was the first of her kind. If you can dream her up, Eve was that, a God-fashioned "WOW-man."

Adam hadn't touched her or spoken to her, he had only seen her and all this energy was generated. Some people say that Eve's great beauty was the reason Adam was distracted from keeping the garden as he should have. That may or may not have been the reason that precipitated the Fall, but Eve did listen to the serpent's suggestion to go ahead and eat from the Tree of the Knowledge of Good and Evil. Then Adam listened to Eve's suggestion and ate from the tree, even though God had explicitly told him not to eat from it.

But keep in mind that the garden was home for the man. His work was dressing and tending to his home. Now the question must be asked, how did the serpent make his way into the garden? At what point is it okay for a serpent or demon to take up residence in your home? The serpent was an inhabitant of the field, not a resident of the garden. When did Adam leave his responsibility of keeping the garden and allow a field beast to roam free in his home?

In like manner, when did man stop being the watchman on the wall of his home? Who told him that God's order had changed? Who told him to stop protecting and guarding? We, like Adam, think it nothing to leave the responsibility God has given us, yielding to the persuasion of our own desires. In many cases, we turn our God-appointed position over to the "Eve" He has given us. And when we find ourselves out of our designed place, we fail to see how foolish we look when we turn and blame the woman.

The woman was and is a blessing to the man. She is a gift given by God Himself. Your God-given call to have and keep a relationship with the Father is not changed due to the arrival of the woman. On the contrary, her arrival brings more responsibility and should drive you to a deeper relationship with God as you now need to know how to love and interact with this woman. Thus, man's orders haven't changed since Adam. We are still dressing, keeping, and loving as God commands.

I was speaking with my friend Darryl, and discussing the amount of continuing education courses my wife had to take to stay certified in her field compared to those I had to take to maintain my license. He was surprised at the frequency of all the classes we had to take, and the amount of information to be studied and comprehended. I explained that each industry was in a constant state of change, which required constant study to stay relevant. After a long pause, Darryl commented, "I pray each day for God to give me what it takes to love my wife; because marriage changes from day to day.

Darryl was expressing that what he needs to love his wife today may very well have changed from what he used yesterday; therefore, he requires a fresh download from Heaven daily of how to truly love her. Darryl understands that the love industry is in a state of constant change. He also understands that his wife's needs change as do his own; therefore, fresh instruction is necessary if we are to be current in today's climate.

> "He can't hurt me intentionally and he must fill a need."
> —Evelyn Dickson

CHAPTER 6

Adam Was There

YES, HE WAS right there. As the serpent was speaking with Adam's beautiful wife, Adam just stood there. The scripture explicitly points out that after Eve took and ate the fruit of the Tree of the Knowledge of Good and Evil, "she also gave to her husband ***with her***, and he ate" (Genesis 3:6, emphasis added). But Adam said nothing to Eve nor to the serpent. Why didn't he just speak to the serpent? After all, Adam had been given authority by God to have dominion over the animals. Why did he allow Eve to be enticed, tempted, and persuaded? Perhaps this could be why one of a woman's greatest concerns is being left to navigate hostile situations in her own frailty, worried that her man would just remain silent and do nothing to protect her should she ever be threatened.

Again, read Genesis 3:1-6. A beast of the field is in Adam's home, speaking to his wife. He is right there, but says and does nothing until after the fact.

Without recounting the entire story, we know that the serpent approached Eve to tempt her to eat the forbidden fruit. The surprising thing is that she didn't have to go looking for Adam. It would also be tempting to initially give Adam a small pass if he, like a lot of us, was buried in work, other activities, or simply didn't want to be disturbed. However, he was spending time with his lady, which is usually a good thing, but that's where the positives stop.

Ladies relish being defended and protected, as well as being made to feel safe and content. Adam performed none of the above. He did not defend Eve, he did not protect Eve, he did not make her feel safe, and he did not make her feel content. He was right there and said not a word to the intruder. Why is this so surprising? Because of the fact that for most men, laying down their lives is easier for them than spending unplanned time with their wives. Yes, we will fight and defend against any physical threat, but without spending time with her, it will be hard to recognize and then defend against subtle threats. Without taking the time to tend to your wife, you will never learn her signals and signs of an atmosphere change. By the time you wake up, the beast will have already begun to influence her. Or in the worst-case scenario, like with Eve, if you're not paying attention, the enemy may have already deceived her into disobeying God.

When I was employed as an automobile sales manager, I routinely worked sixty-five to seventy hours a week. This schedule really cut into the time my wife and I spent with each other. I tried to cover everybody with the little off time I had. That little bit of time had to be further divided among my wife and children, next came Mom and Dad, and then came church obligations. And what about some "me" time?

This really put a strain on things at home, and one day I came face-to-face with a subtle attack. Like Adam, I never saw it coming and I, like Adam, also failed by saying nothing.

As One: *Like Christ and the Church*

You see, my wife had brought the children to see me at work because, as usual, I was working late. This day we were very busy. Customers were everywhere. Just as I came to the car to speak to my family, one of my coworkers beat me to the car and spoke harshly to my wife, telling her that I was too busy to deal with her and that this was not the time for a visit. Instead of defending her and coming to her rescue, I simply told her, "I'm very busy." I said hello to the girls, and told my wife I'd call her later.

Finishing my long day, I was welcomed home by my wife with a chill and a stare that was so cold. Of course, I didn't know why. After some one-sided conversation because she was not speaking to me, my light bulb finally came on and I apologized. And I apologized some more.

Both my and Adam's failure came in not speaking up. Instead of being the hero of the day, I, like Adam, was left pointing the finger at someone or something else. In my mind, I was working – working for the family. I was in work-mode, not husband-mode. It's easy to recognize why my "husband radar" was down. Yeah, that's what I thought, but there is never a reason for any husband not to protect his wife.

Adam, though with Eve, was not engaged in anything when Eve was approached. Adam was with her and yet distracted. He was distracted so much so that I'm not sure he even knew what fruit Eve handed him, and when asked by God to account for his actions, he dared to point the finger at God for giving him the woman. Even though he had been obedient in dressing and keeping the garden, his focus was so off that he didn't recognize that a formidable threat had walked right into his paradise.

When we get overly occupied with work, friends, family, church, sports, rest, and any number of things, they can take us away from being on point with and for our wives, and an attack is sure to come.

> "He must love me and respect my place in ministry."
> —Yavonnda Mack

CHAPTER 7

Do You Know Her?

TIME SPENT IN study or research of an area gives you knowledge of that area. Enough study or even a mastery of said area could make you an expert. You can also be awarded undergraduate and post-graduate degrees in a field, which indicate one's level of understanding and/or expertise. A man can easily spend twenty, thirty, even forty years in a vocation or job and be considered an expert in his field. But who among us is an expert in his marriage? The question is not, "Are you an expert on marriage?" The question is, "Are you an expert in the field of *your* marriage?"

In most countries, the only requirement for getting married is that of reaching a certain age. There are no required classes or seminars to attend, and no certifications to be obtained. My research did find that certain countries have some additional rules for non-citizens who desire to be married in those countries. There are also some organizations that have their own requirements that must be met before a couple can be married by that particular organization.

But in the United States, there are basically no restrictions for people eighteen years old or older. Since there are no specified requirements, man is left to his own understanding, to figure out this gift of a woman by trial and error...mostly error.

Even knowing all of that, men believe that by some miracle, they are born with this knowledge of women, or that knowledge of women is gained simply by living. This assumption is so far from reality, it's ridiculous. We think we know. We don't feel the need to study our woman. The thought of putting forth intentional effort to research her is all but a waste of time because we already know. We think the small drops of information picked up in our day-to-day contact gives us all we need to navigate the constantly shifting waters of a successful relationship with a woman.

Personal interaction through school, work, and other social outlets has given us a glimpse into the woman's world, but those interactions are truly only a peek into all she is. Even some early relationships, such as interactions in coworker or social settings, have given us some limited idea of how to relate to a woman. But as any woman will tell you, what may have worked for you in dealing with other ladies will not work for her because she will tell you, "You don't know me."

Before going on, let's see how well you can answer the questions below.

Do you know your wife?

1. When is her birthday?
2. Can you do it before she asks you (whatever "IT" may be)?
3. When is your anniversary?
4. What is her favorite restaurant?
5. What is her favorite food?
6. What type(s) of music does she like?
7. Who is her favorite artist?

8. Who is her favorite group?
9. What is her favorite concert venue?
10. Does she like sports? If so, what/who is her favorite team/athlete?
11. What is her favorite hobby?
12. How does she relax?
13. Is she a bargain shopper?
14. What is her taste in shoes, clothes, and/or jewelry?
15. What are her favorite stores?
16. Is she cold-natured or hot-natured?
17. Does she like compliments?
18. Are hugs important?
19. What is the best dish she cooks or bakes?
20. Does she enjoy flowers, cards, and/or candy?
21. Can you order for her if she's not at the table?
22. What is her favorite color?
23. What signals indicate that she's tired?
24. Does she prefer love stories, dramas, or comedies?
25. What is her favorite movie?
26. Will she show emotion while watching a movie?

27. Does she prefer indoor or outdoor activities?
28. Does she prefer the beach or the city?
29. Is she an early riser or late sleeper?
30. Does she prefer a good book or social media?
31. Does she like your family?
32. Does she like her own family?

So, how did you do? There are so many more areas that could be covered here like questions about finances, politics, religion, and more, but you get the point. Knowing your wife is not some new thing. Adam was faced with this from the beginning.

"And Adam knew Eve his wife; and she conceived, and bare Cain, and said, 'I have gotten a man from the LORD'" (Genesis 4:1).

The word "know" in this passage refers to sexual intimacy, but it is also a "knowing" which carries a much deeper intimacy than the sexual act. Truth be told, it is easily and entirely possible for men to have sex and there be no intimacy at all, so how dare we attempt to box God in and limit His meaning to the physical (intercourse)?

To truly know a woman takes work, passion, and commitment. You see, knowing your wife carries a much deeper meaning than sex, and you need to be ever studying and learning about her, because graduation only comes when Christ returns.

You must, as a man, take note of each and every detail. Each nuance of movement, emotion, glance, or smile can have a different meaning. With each new day class begins and continues. Just when you think you have really learned something, the Teacher (Father God) introduces a new lesson to you by way of your wife, and today that glance, smile, or raised brow carries a new meaning.

You must be ever ready for the next lesson.

These lessons are good for the man in that they keep him on full alert. Alert for what, you may ask? Alert to any change of temperature, and especially alert to any beast of the field trying to make its way into your home.

This state of readiness fits directly into the makeup of the man, for we were made for adventure, challenge, quest, and conquest. Therefore, I ask you, brother of mine, what better adventure to be faced with than continual discovery of the wonderful woman with whom you've chosen to become one?

> "I should imitate the love I see in Christ and give my life for her. I left my family to marry her because with her is where I had to be."
>
> —Carlos McGee

CHAPTER 8

The 100 Percenter

MANHOOD DOESN'T JUST fall on you like rain. Maturity doesn't just happen. The time comes when every boy must "man up" on purpose, and the man up position is not for the faint of heart; neither is marriage. Entering both maturity and manhood is for the big boys. Issues come first because you are alive. Life happens! To complicate matters, we have men apprehended in adolescence taking on man-sized responsibilities and God-sized assignments for which they are not prepared. They are arrested, as it seems, in adolescence, unable to demonstrate accountability or any resemblance of true manhood.

Our society (through magazines, television, sitcoms, songs on the radio, music videos, etc.) has caused

As One: *Like Christ and the Church*

men and women to accept a 50 percent role in marriage. This is especially true when either one is defending his or her ground. We are quick to say, "Marriage is fifty-fifty; I got my part, he/she should take care of his/her part." There is some level of truth in this statement, since men and women can never fully replace one another. Even though circumstances and situations may dictate that we act as both father and mother, this is not God's original design.

Marriage is a God-sized endeavor to be undertaken with faith, prayer, vision, help, and hope. A godly marriage sets out to operate undergirded by the godly standard, which does not include a fifty-fifty proposition.

The concept of a fifty-fifty relationship opens the door for either spouse to be less than what God created him or her to be. Marriage is not a fifty-fifty partnership. Marriage is not a fifty-fifty agreement. Marriage is not a fifty-fifty anything. Marriage is a 100/100 percent relationship.

The husband must be 100 percent man, and the wife must be 100 percent woman. The wife should not be looking for the husband to complete her, and the husband should not be looking for the wife to complete him. If you are not complete in yourself and in God, no woman will complete you. This is not the reason to pursue a wife. Your mate should be someone who will enhance you and assist in your completing the assignment God has given you on the earth.

The 100 percent man is a man of God with the mind of Christ, always seeking to please the Father. He is a man who will search out the heart of the Father. Then he sets his mind and heart to align with God's will thereafter. A 100 percent man imitates Christ and says as Jesus said in John 5:30, "I can of Myself do nothing. As I hear, I judge; and My judgment is righteous, because I do not seek My own will but the will of the Father who sent Me" (NKJ). Jesus was about His Father's business. In John 4:34, the Savior says, "My food is to do the will of Him who sent Me, and to finish His work" (NKJ). He accepted the position and assignment given Him by the Father, and the 100 percent man must do the same.

The God-man is a 100 percenter who will seek the Father's plan. He will seek the Father's will, and he will seek the Father. He will discover why he was placed on the earth now and in his marriage. He will ask what to do, where to go, when to speak, or when to hold his peace. He is like Christ in that he will see the joy that is set before him as he walks in obedience to his Father. He runs this race with patience. Hebrews 12:1-2 spells out this concept:

> "Therefore, since we are surrounded by such a huge crowd of witnesses to the life of faith, let us strip off every weight that slows us down, especially the sin that so easily trips us up. And let us run with endurance (translated "run with patience" in the King James version) the race God has set before us. We do this by keeping our eyes on Jesus, the champion who initiates and perfects our faith. Because of the joy awaiting him, he endured the cross, disregarding its shame. Now he is seated in the place of honor beside God's throne" (NLT).

You see, not only are these the traits that please the Father, they are also the traits a woman looks for in a man. She wants a man with dreams and aspirations, goals, and vision. She wants a man who will lead her against the world and into a brave new world that they are to explore together. A woman enjoys that place in her husband where there is safety and contentment. In that atmosphere, she will flourish and blossom.

The 100 percenter understands this. The 100 percenter expects this to be his life. He also knows that he is nothing without the leading and direction of the Holy Spirit. His heart's cry is "Lord, teach me to love this woman."

> "He must be a divine covering; providing everything righteous and holy."
>
> —Kathrine Adams

CHAPTER 9

My Story

I WAS MARRIED at the age of twenty-three to my college sweetheart. We were just wide-eyed and open for the adventure of a lifetime. After a few years and a few children, our adventure became more of a grind. Food, electricity, diapers, and formula seemed to be what life had given us to look forward to. I remember the day the last child was done needing diapers! Wow, one less bill. Yes, that's how I viewed those diapers; another bill.

As time moved on we continued the day-to-day grind. It was a challenge to say the least, but we could always find a reason to smile. When you don't have much, a trip to the park knowing the lights will be on when you return was a treat. Through all of this, we relied on love and the Lord, but after a time, our love began to crack.

My wife began to suffer from low self-esteem, loneliness, lack of achievement, and overall homesickness. She chose to medicate with alcohol.

We began to make more money and get a better footing financially, but this also meant she had more money to indulge in her habit. Alcohol began to take over our home.

I held on to faith and hope, because she and I were in covenant with God. That covenant with God was my non-negotiable. I had to fight for my wife. I had to fight for my family. I had to fight for our life. Losing was not an option.

To bring you into my world, I must give you a few more details. I was working a lot and she was drinking a lot. Most nights when I got home, she was asleep with her drink next to the bed. Then there was the burning of pots on the stove, wrecking the car by hitting the house, and having the girls in the car while intoxicated. During all this I never thought of leaving, never thought of taking the girls and leaving my wife to handle this for herself.

My Story

I set up arrangements for rehab clinics that she refused to enter. I changed bank accounts so she couldn't have easy access to money. All the while, prayer and fasting for my family was taking place.

By the time we were into this addiction for about ten years, other family members were asking me to leave my wife. My answer was always the same; I was in covenant with this woman. A longtime friend begged me to get out and said there was no way any man should have to live with this. I said that "I'm not any man. I am her husband and you aren't." My hope was real and I wasn't going to be talked out of it.

After living in the situation for some fifteen years, I have to admit that I was tired. The girls were tired. I was to the point that prayer was even hard. I remember speaking to a minister friend of mine and telling him that I could pray for anything and any situation, but I could no longer pray for her. I was out of words.

By this point we were all addicts in the sense that we had all been affected and had adjusted our lives to cope with the monster that was this addiction. We had adjusted to keeping the peace, because if she wasn't intoxicated, she was angry. Because I worked so much, her anger would be directed toward the girls. They learned to avoid her as much as they could. The verbal abuse was constant. I learned ways to get them to safer places and activities whenever possible.

Alcoholism was winning, it seemed. I also made some uncharacteristic choices that led to much self-examination. She was drinking and I was not sure who I was anymore.

The craziest thing about all this was that I continued to look for her deliverance. I had dreams of the retreats, conferences, and marriage workshops we would host. Our testimony would be such a representation of the power and grace of God. Her response was always the same, "Boy, you crazy. I can't wait to get out of here." I'd laugh and say she couldn't see it, but it was coming.

Finally, the only way to be free was to get free, so we divorced. I came to understand that she also had a free will, and not even God would violate that. It was time to move on. I was as damaged by alcohol as she was, without my ever taking a drink.

Being a percenter, that's what I knew I'd given: 100 percent. I'd fought and prayed longer than I could even believe. It was time to let go.

If there were any should haves or could haves, they were because of the girls. My staying for as long as I did also caused the girls to experience many disappointments, and it also has given them a fight that they are just now discovering.

> "He must be the priest of his home who looks out for his family and works hard. He keeps God first and family second with an eye always on the future."
> —Stephanie McKinney

CHAPTER 10
The 100 Percenter Continued

THE 100 PERCENTER will go above and beyond the norm. Who set normal for us all anyway? To be a 100 percenter, the measure of normal is best found in, and indeed can only be found in the example of Christ. To work through rejection, ridicule, separation, false accusations, and much more shows the likeness of Christ. He endured so much to redeem us so we could be His bride.

The 100 percenter is a warrior, a constant winner, and protective watchman. But he doesn't stop there. He is also a man who provides finances, shelter, food, transportation, and all the other necessities of physical life, along with friendship, comfort, a kind word, tenderness, and care.

He is a teacher of the Word, a man of praise, and a true worshiper of God. The 100 percenter is a man of prayer and counsel. He never runs from his God-given responsibilities, but takes counsel with the Father for understanding and guidance.

Christ taught His followers the ways of the Father. The 100 percent man must do the same for his wife and family. He must teach her the ways and Word of the Father even more than the deeds of the Father.

She may have been a disciple of Christ longer than her husband, and at this moment may have more biblical knowledge. She may have been to Bible school and every convention and conference offered, but none of this takes the place of the life of Christ she desires to see and needs to see in her husband. No outside conversation or study of the Word will go deeper for a wife than that which she has with her husband. Mr. 100 percent will go after knowledge and wisdom with a vengeance because he knows he is the head of that house and he

The 100 Percenter Continued

must lead. And when you chase God in this way, He will be found.

Dr. Michael Freeman asked a poignant question after facing a near-death experience. He asked, "If your life depended on the Word of God that you have poured into your wife, would you live or would you die?"

Wow! You're in an Intensive Care Unit and the only thing that can save you are the prayers and confessions of your wife. Your hopes rest in the seed of faith your wife has stored, which has increased only because of how much you've watered that seed. Your direct interaction in the Word with her is your key to victory. What is your confidence level at this point? What are your odds? Are you confident in the Word that you have poured into your wife?

Let's consider your place of worship. Are you confident that her seed of faith can blossom there as God designed? She must now thrive in that soil without you there to cover her. Is that a nurturing environment or one filled with toxins? She is your beautiful flower and you must be positive she finds the best environment possible.

This makes it real. I ask again, how confident are you in the Word you've poured into your wife? I pray that you'd make it.

This is one area of marriage that is so neglected. Many husbands have never even given consideration to the thought that the spiritual climate of his home is his responsibility. Let's lighten that up a bit. We men are charged, equipped, and trusted by God to lead the spiritual growth of our families. The God of the universe has chosen you and gifted you for the enjoyment of this endeavor.

I hear you saying that that's way too much pressure. That's only because you don't understand on whom the pressure truly lies. The real pressure is squarely on God.

He created you and placed you in this position; therefore, it's on Him to teach you and fill you with His Word. As you attend services and group studies, as you read the Word and truly think about it, God must bring you revelation and understanding. More than that, nothing brings Him more joy than seeing

The 100 Percenter Continued

His handiwork – you and your wife in marriage – operating as you were created to operate.

Question is, are you ready for the download? Will you open yourself to the vastness of possibilities that being a husband has to offer? You've signed up for this Real Man position. There is nothing left except to man up!

"Dedicated and devoted to that one woman."
—Thelma Mapps

CHAPTER 11

A Good Man - The Provider

"But if anyone does not provide for his relatives, and especially for members of his household, he has denied the faith and is worse than an unbeliever" (1 Timothy 5:8).

WHEN WE THINK of man as provider, we automatically think of the work that man does or the career that man has. We see each man as having a job or profession that provides finance, food, clothing, and shelter for himself and his family. Handling these provisions used to be all one had to do to be considered "a good man."

But today, providing has expanded to include vacations, college, 401(k)s, and more. And we agree that all these categories fall under the mantle of provider, but are there more? Are these things even the most important or primary things for the provider to provide? Or are they simply the path that is easily set for a young man? In my conversations with both men and women, I've learned how much women value a man who will clean her car, pump the gas, take out the trash, and open the door for her. These tasks may seem small, but doing the little things makes a woman know her man is able to handle the big things, so don't take them for granted.

Jesus was teaching and said these words:

> "Therefore, I tell you, do not be anxious about your life, what you will eat or what you will drink, nor about your body, what you will put on. Is not life more than food and the body more than clothing?
>
> Look at the birds of the air: they neither sow nor reap nor gather into barns, and yet your heavenly Father feeds them. Are you not of more value than them?

A Good Man - The Provider

And which of you by being anxious can add a single hour to his span of life?

And why are you anxious about clothing? Consider the lilies of the field, how they grow: they neither toil nor spin, Yet I tell you, even Solomon in all his glory was not arrayed like one of these.

But if God so clothes the grass of the field, which today is alive and tomorrow is thrown into the oven, will he not much more clothe you, O you of little faith?

Therefore, do not be anxious, saying, 'What shall we eat?' or 'What shall we drink?' or 'What shall we wear?' For the Gentiles seek after all these things, and your heavenly Father knows that you need them all. But seek first the kingdom of God and his righteousness, and all these things will be added to you" (Matthew 6:25-33).

Men are taught from a young age to work at something. They are taught to get an education and then acquire a job or start a business that will provide for themselves and their future families.

Jesus led the hungry disciples through a field and they ate of the grain of that field on the Sabbath day.

As One: *Like Christ and the Church*

I am referencing this story not only to show that Jesus knows we must eat natural food, but also because the pursuit of the Kingdom is of utmost importance (spiritual food and life).

And who better to lead in this pursuit of the Kingdom than the one set as head of the house? Husbands are to lead in the study of the Word. They should regularly bring up topics and questions of Kingdom importance for discussion. (We'll discuss this more when we discuss how husbands are also priests in their homes.)

Let's get back to the money. The man should make the money, right? He should control the money, right? And the wife should defer to her husband about money matters, right?

These are all former norms. Yes, these are former and outdated mind-sets and models that are still accepted as the primary way a household should function. But the longer we live, the easier it is to see the changing landscape of the family. Many of you may be like me, that even in your most productive income year, your wife still makes more money. In this case, who should control the finances?

A Good Man - The Provider

This is a very important question that needs to be answered in each home. If left to former norms, without real discussion and agreement, this question becomes a huge issue. Yes, this is an issue that comes up week after week and eventually becomes a real point of division. So how should this be handled?

In our home, where my wife brings in a greater income than I do, we didn't wait for finances to become an issue. We attacked this subject from the very beginning. We first decided that there would be no such thing as "my money" and "her money." There are no secret or separate individual accounts. Joint accounts encourage transparency and unity. All income belongs to the house. We are both working toward the greater good and benefit of the family.

We discuss all large purchases and what we judge to be major decisions. The week-to-week and month-to-month bill pay is my responsibility. I handle this because it gives my wife comfort in not having to be faced with this task. She operates from day to day in peace, because she knows I've got our household monetary issues handled.

Most money matters will be routine and not require any real discussion. Most of our debts are predictable. All the while I'm managing our finances, my wife is kept informed of balances and any changes. She loves it when I say, "It's paid in full." When the weightier issues arise, my wife and I come together and find agreement to resolve the matter. We never strike out alone. This works in our home.

You may opt for individual accounts for personal disposable income as many couples do. Be careful with these accounts. Each account should be reviewed from time to time in order to maintain transparency.

A lot of men don't do well when their wives make a higher income because men gain so much of their self-esteem and self-worth from their incomes. I have been asked many times how I handle my wife being the primary breadwinner. My answer is simple, quick, and always the same, "I love it!"

You have a truly pathetic view of yourself if you only see yourself as a paycheck. The sad truth is that this is the way most men are taught. Being a responsible man by running your business, being in public service, or working in industry will supply you with a great deal of satisfaction. So, why is that satisfaction diminished because your wife has a larger salary? This sort of attitude only produces feelings of personal doubt and causes you to focus only on your inadequacies. If these doubts continue to fester and grow, they can then produce resentment and rivalry within the relationship. Now, instead of loving her, covering her, and being her hero, you are her chief combatant. This will never work. So, ask yourself these questions: Who am I without my job? What do I have to give other than my salary? What is my value to my family if my wife makes more money than I do?

You see, we're not speaking of someone who's lazy and just being a dope. No, that lazy man doesn't care so long as he's being provided for. We're talking about the man who struggles with pride or embarrassment when his wife has the larger income. We're talking about the man who feels small because his wife is in the spotlight instead of him. It would be easy to say that this is a silly, even immature attitude and life view, but it is real. When a man doesn't know who he is, it is easy for his ego to blind him of the blessing God has provided for the house. This blessing just so happens to come through the vessel of his wife.

So how do we fight this and win? How do we keep this beast of the field from coming into our garden? We must first know who we are in Christ. We must learn what the God of all creation says about us and then believe it. Believe it! Yes, believe it!

Next, learn what you do bring to the family besides your income.

If income is all you are, what will you do when life happens? Layoffs, downsizing, businesses lost or sold, changes in the market, even sickness: all of these are commonplace, and one or all could happen. You must be more than your income or the family will be deficient. So, believe it. Say it with me:

I AM MORE THAN MY INCOME! PRAISE GOD!

Having a man in place in the home brings foundation. He is the solid point of contact for the rest of the family. Even though he may not make each and every decision on daily activities, his foundational presence gives his wife the confidence to do so. He provides a safe place for the family to function without worry or fear.

Wisdom and sound judgment are also attributes provided by a good man. Women count on their husbands keeping their cool and being the practical thinkers. Your practicality makes it safe for her to express her emotion freely, knowing that you are there to comfort her and walk with her through any situation.

Unfortunately, there exists a negative possibility to the above scenario. This happens when the husband brings whatever he makes home and gives it to the wife; however, along with the check, he dumps all of the obligations on her. This husband feels he is then free to do whatever pleases him. Since he frees himself of any responsibility as to the financial health of the home, this man is now released to digress to that place of no worries or concerns. And what has he accomplished? He has provided, right? Absolutely not! All he's done is made some money and brought it home, but he left all the stress of financial management on his wife.

Regrettably, this is the practice of many a man. This practice is usually fine so long as the money is long and the trouble is short. But what happens if a crisis occurs? The husband assumes no responsibility because he gave it all to the wife. And please don't underestimate the added emotional stress that she will experience. This has the potential to cause major conflict, especially if blame and finger pointing come into the picture.

Now it is not a put-down on the husband if the wife is best at handling the finances for their household. Gone are the days when a man who is terrible with money is still expected to control financial things simply because he is male. The concerned husband and true provider, even if he's bad with numbers, will with his wife, work toward a solution to the financial issues in their lives together. Yes, together.

A pastor friend of mine freely admits that his wife handles the household finances. When asked what he'd do if she were out of commission for a time, he said he'd gladly defer to his adult children. For his home, this decision for his wife to manage the finances for now, and in the event of some incident where she wasn't able, to

A Good Man - The Provider

defer to his children, brings peace to all involved. This works for his home.

Each family needs to put in real work and have purposeful discussion concerning their money management, absent of ego and pride. Remember that regardless of who manages the money, you as the husband have still been placed as the head of that family. You're the one on whom God laid the leadership responsibility. The restful place here is in knowing that since God placed the responsibility of leadership upon you, He will also supply the resources and skills for success. Our place as men is to seek and trust Him for all the answers we need.

As stated earlier, the husband provides more than finances. He also provides peace and contentment in the home. He is that safe place.

As a boy, when I wasn't in any trouble, it was always a joy when Daddy got home. He could build or fix anything. Many a lesson was learned by just observing him. The atmosphere of the home changed when Dad got home. My mom loved to say, "Wait till your Dad gets home."

As One: *Like Christ and the Church*

When my girls were young they couldn't wait for me to get home. Our routine was for me to come in, put my things down, lay on the floor, and allow them to jump all over me. Kissing, punching, squeezing, tickling, and anything else they thought of was fair game. This is how they greeted me and we all loved it until they were, in their minds, too old for the game anymore. But when I came home, all things were well.

"If he loves God, he will automatically love me."
—Darlene Pinson

CHAPTER 12

A Good Man - The Priest

BEING THE PRIEST in the home can be one of the most rewarding positions to which a man is called. This position removes ego, pride, self-righteousness, and self-dependence. As the priest of the home, the husband becomes the primary example of a godly servant.

We have heard for centuries the stories of the praying grandmother and of the mom who stayed up all night with the ailing child. These depictions are relevant and true, but they are not the whole story. Fathers share in praying for and caring for the children.

My youngest daughter grew up with asthma. This landed her in the emergency room more than a few times. I would usually stay overnight with her. When

As One: *Like Christ and the Church*

I heard her tell a friend of the comfort she felt when she'd wake at two or three o'clock in the morning and I was sitting at the foot of her bed, it made me feel like Super Dad. I'd pray for her and play gospel music, the same things we'd do at home from time to time.

The spiritual atmosphere of the home should be set by the priest, and the father in every home is the priest. Temple priests were appointed by God to serve His people. They performed all the temple rituals and ceremonies. In other words, the priest served the people as they came to the temple. They were also charged with the care of the temple furnishings and supplies.

The priest is not just an example of a servant, but he is a true servant. His position, given to him by God, is to serve. These duties are so important to God that the priest was not given an inheritance of property in the Promised Land. What he received was to come solely from the service he rendered.

Likewise, as the priest in your home, no one should out-serve you in your home. The service you give your wife and children should be unmatched. Your service encourages the children by what they see in your example. Your children will brag on you, encouraged by the thought that nothing will ever deter their dad.

As a servant, you seek no self-gratification or reward. Your compensation is that of a home engulfed in peace and love, a home that is set in order. The order of the home is in direct correspondence to your deep love for God and your desire to please Him. This desire to please your Heavenly Father is in no way demonstrated more than by how you serve and love your wife.

Because you love God and are in relationship with Him, you serve Him. I realize that we've been taught for years that the wife sets the tone for the home. I disagree. The degree to which any wife can set the tone for the home is in direct relation to the love and care she receives from you, her husband. This atmosphere of love is set by you, the priest, and instilled throughout the home.

So, are you being her priest? How do you care for her spiritually? You heard me right, brother. How do *you* care for her?

Let's look at some examples that show how true care for your wife is achieved. As simple as these solutions will sound, they are very difficult for many men to do. Why? Because of pride and ego mainly, and we understand that these are both signs of selfishness. Some men just don't believe they are qualified, but God knows both you and your spouse; therefore, He has equipped you for this. So, take a deep breath, and start.

1. Pray both for her and with her. You be the one to set specific times for prayer, fasting, and personal consecration for the family.

Regular prayer will bring an openness to your marriage that most couples never experience. By praying for and with her, you are allowing her to hear your heart.

And for as much as she is open to you, she will discover new places in herself to be free and expressive. Why? Because you give her permission as you reveal the tenderness of your heart in prayer.

2. Be the leader in Bible reading. Select a book for the month to read. Start out by just reading it. Don't be concerned with explanation, just read. You can always

follow a reading plan from an app on the many devices at our disposal. One of the easiest is to read a chapter in Proverbs each day, as there are thirty-one chapters. That gives you one chapter for each day of the month for most months. Read the chapter and then each of you can discuss a verse that was special to you from the reading.

3. Get a copy of each week's message from your church and review it. Listen to it again together and take notes. After listening, discuss each other's points of interest. This exercise could also spawn questions for further study. Allow God to take you deeper in the Word together.

4. Study a word such as faith, love, or hope. Or even choose a topic like why we fast, the creation story, or maybe study a biblical person of interest like David, Moses, Esther, and/or others.

5. Be proactive with your wife and family by really paying attention to the comments and concerns they may

express about a message or a news story. This is your material for other study and discussion times. Search the Bible and connect current events to the Word of God. The beauty of this is that no matter your experience with the scriptures, focusing on what they are interested in and the events around you will show your family how relevant and timely God's Word is. Simultaneously, each family member will see and hear how important they are to you. They'll know that you heard them and you are willing to take the time to bring their cares and concerns to the forefront.

At the time of this writing I was a part of a Facebook® discussion and thought it would be good to share these thoughts. Check it out:

September 1 at 8:12p.m.

Question: Do you care if your spouse or significant other loves you? WARNING: This is an exercise in critical thinking....

Answer: Yes...

A Good Man - The Priest

Q: Why? And how do you know they care?

A: I want to know that I'm loved by the person I've chosen to spend the rest of my life with. I guess I know I care because if I had any doubt about them loving me it would bother me.

Q: Do you care that they love you or that they behave like they do?

A: Both, honestly...

Other reply: Doesn't he or she have to care about you before they could love you? Yes, it matters if they care for you but if you find out otherwise just leave, that person isn't for you.

Other reply: Jesus said that the world will know that you are my disciples by your love for one another. So, there is definitely value in loving someone in word and in deed. It reveals the God in you. And since the union between man and wife mirrors that of Christ and His bride it fulfills a deep purpose.

Q: So, are we talking about love behavior and not feelings (which was really the essence of my question)?

Other reply: I've been thinking about this question and honestly how do you know if someone loves you? By their actions. Love in marriage is a verb not a noun. So yes, I care if you treat me like you love me.

Questioner's reply: That's what I say too. I care if you treat me like you love me.

Other reply: I've yet to see somebody treat somebody lovingly and loving feelings are not engendered especially within the context of marriage.

As the discussion went on, I had to join.

Reggie Holder (RH): While both are expressed in action, the greatest need for a woman is love, whereas the greatest need for a man is respect. See Ephesians 5:33.

Q: What is the difference when you consider behavior?

RH: A man can really care less if you tell him that you love him. Most women need to hear the words as well as see the actions of love. Respecting the man is loving the man. Lift him up, comment on his value to you and he will run through walls for you, walls you would never get knocked down if you have never said you love him.

Q: What I am asking is if neither party could use words, *behaviorally*, what is the difference? Is there one?

RH: The difference is most ladies need to hear the words. Men always say, I wouldn't do all I do if I didn't love you.

As One: *Like Christ and the Church*

Q: Um...so, in your opinion and experience, a woman would prefer hearing the words to seeing the actions? Or if she sees the actions, she wouldn't recognize them as love until she hears the words?

RH: For total fulfillment the words must accompany the actions. The words are so important because so many men have trouble expressing them. Men would rather do than say.

Questioner's reply: Ok. Thanks for the feedback.

At this point I thought we were done, but the Questioner's wheels were still turning.

Q: Ok...so if a woman wants to hear the words more, what will a woman do if a man freely tells her he loves her but treats her badly? Or if a man doesn't tell her but treats her in ways she always dreamed about?

RH: First know that the actions are always the truth. True love is always most deeply expressed in action. In the second case, she will have to know her man and not push him too much for those words of affirmation. He just may not be a verbal person. But please receive the dream treatment. It's the truth.

What drew me in was the presence of the need to be loved, as expressed by the participants in this discussion. There are various ways this is achieved depending on the individual; nevertheless, the need most certainly exists.

Most of this discussion was centered around the premise, "Do you see me, do you hear me, and do I matter enough to get your real attention?"

When the priest is present in the home, there is no doubt. These qualities will be on display for the world to see. Brothers, take your place in the tabernacle of your home. No one can fill your shoes.

"He must love God more than he loves me."
—Rose Crowder

CHAPTER 13

A Good Man - The Prophet

MY FRIEND DEREK Young of Derek Young Speaks is a corporate trainer, executive coach, motivational speaker, husband, and father. He says that every family must have a plan. More to the point, he says that the father should be the point man in initiating this plan. Derek believes every family needs an annual plan, a three-year, a five-year, a ten-year plan, and a retirement plan.

When these plans are in place, there is no confusion as to where the family is headed and what's expected of each member. Your plan can be long or short, that is up to you, but you must formulate a family plan. Start

As One: *Like Christ and the Church*

with a simple outline. As you seek God's direction for your family, He will fill in the details. For most men, their wives will be impressed simply because you are thinking this way. Your wife will then be inspired to seek God even more for the future of her family and ways she can contribute to the plan.

There is one thing that must be a part of your family plan and that is purpose. More specifically, the purpose of God has to be figured in to the family plan. Truly, before we make any plans, we should seek the purpose of God for our family. Once the purpose is revealed, then our plans should be made to coincide with that known purpose.

We are taught in this great society of ours, "Don't just sit there, do something." To the contrary, Henry Blackaby, author of *Experiencing God*, teaches, "Don't just do something, sit there. Sit there until you've heard from God. We must be active in pursuit of the will of God. His will is not something we just stumble upon. We must meditate and ponder in prayer and thought that we may know the will of our Father."

A Good Man - The Prophet

Can you imagine what life would be like if every man sought after God this way? Think of how fabulous family life would be if every man waited to find the plan and purpose of God for himself and his family even before he got married. What a driven, enlightened, peaceful, and adventure-filled life this mind-set could lead to, knowing that each day could be attacked with the knowledge of the will of God. Wow!

Some of you are saying to yourselves, *What's this got to do with being the prophet in the home?* I'm glad that question came up in your minds. The answer is that seeking out God's purpose has everything to do with being the prophet in your home. The fully equipped man is one who has heard from God, gathered the plan of God, and then effectively conveys that plan to his bride and his family.

We are so used to church definitions of things that falling back on those often off-base definitions causes us to miss walking in the fullness of our callings and appointments. When we see the word "prophet," lots of ideas come to mind along with a ton of excuses. The main excuses that I've heard all over the country are,

As One: Like Christ and the Church

"I'm not deep enough or versed enough for the role of prophet," or the best is, "Don't put the title of 'prophet' on me."

Prophet carries many meanings and some are listed here. A prophet is:

- a person chosen to speak for God and to guide the people;
- a person who speaks for God or a deity, or by divine inspiration; and
- a person who foretells or predicts what is to come.

As father and head of a family, aren't these the prophetic duties you perform? Yes? Really?

For example, how many of us have said to our teenager, "No, you can't go with that group because they're trouble"? Were you not speaking under inspiration because you just knew? You could just feel it. That's the prophet in you.

Dad, you are to direct the people God has given you to lead. Dad, you are to recognize and identify the gifts in all your children and speak to the positive future which lies ahead of them.

A Good Man - The Prophet

Husband, you are to cultivate the gifts and talents which are embodied in your wife. You are to make the ground so fertile that even those things she doubts about herself have room to grow. (See Proverbs 31:28-29.)

Simply put, in your place as the family head, you receive God's principles, purpose, and plans, then you proceed to relay them to those He's placed in your care. You give the family a forecast of things to come. You spell out for them their future.

Don't complicate it any more than that. There is no mountain to climb, no giant to slay, and no army to defeat to qualify for this position. There's not even a devil to fight. James 4:7 says, "So humble yourselves before God. Resist the devil, and he will flee from you." There is only a God to humble yourself before.

Self is our toughest foe. That is why the passage first deals with the humbling of self before God. Notice it says that we must do this. Now let's drop the ego and remove the pride and go before God on behalf of our families. If we ask He will answer. If we seek we will find. That's God's promise.

Man, your family is longing to hear from God through you. They are waiting to hear and to know their purpose. The responsibility of this is in your hands, but before you feel the weight of it, take the weight of this truth. God has equipped you for the journey and your success will bring glory to Him. Take that with you. You never walk alone.

> "He must understand the depth of Christ's love so he is equipped to love the entire woman."
>
> —Tangie Jones

CHAPTER 14

To Nourish and to Cherish

A POPULAR ACTOR/TALK show host who likes to give relationship advice made the statement that when a man is "all in" with a woman, he will perform the "Three Ps": profess, provide, and protect.

He states that a man will first profess his love for his lady. He will make this statement first to himself, and second to his lady. Maybe, more importantly, he will profess his devotion and love for her to his family and his friends.

This step is huge for most men, but especially for men who were accustomed to short-term relationships. Think how vulnerable this guy is when his past says that most of his friends never knew if he was even

As One: *Like Christ and the Church*

dating. Now he announces that this particular, special lady is "the one."

Next, he will do all he can to provide for her. He will hold down two or three jobs at a time if necessary. As a matter of fact, it is expected.

Consider this: while little girls were playing "house" and "dress up," little boys were being taught to work. In cases where the father was not around, he was being taught that one day he would take care of his mom who was sacrificing so much for him. Oh yes, he will provide.

Lastly, he will make every effort to protect and keep his loved ones out of harm's way. He will make sure the car is serviced, everything in the home is in good working order, and assure the security of said home. Whether by alarm, baseball bat, or firearm, protection is a given.

As any man opens himself to focus on these three attributes (profess, provide, and protect) to someone other than himself, he's sure this unbridled selflessness is enough to bring any woman and any family all that could ever be needed. Yet, I submit to you that something is missing.

What's missing? The missing ingredient is the heart of the matter; that is, the heart of the man. But wait a minute, you say. We've got men unveiling themselves in three major areas and still you say that something is missing? Yes.

Remember that the marriage relationship is compared to that of Christ and the Church. Christ didn't come to fulfill orders or simply complete the requirements, He came to reconcile us to God and to give us the heart of the Father. Most of us are familiar with John 3:16 which expresses the Father's love for humanity. Love is also the need of every woman. She needs the heartfelt love from the heart of her husband.

Again, the message of Ephesians 5 continues in verses 28 and 29:

"So, ought men to love their wives as their own bodies. He that loveth his wife loveth himself. For no man ever yet hated his own flesh; but nourisheth and cherisheth it, even as the Lord the church."

As One: *Like Christ and the Church*

"Nourish and cherish" sounds like much more than a surface relationship. When a man truly nourishes his wife, he operates in the "to have and to hold" portion of the traditional marriage vows. To put it plainly, he literally holds her, hugs her, nurtures and feeds her mind and emotions.

When we cherish our wives, we put the cherry on top of the sundae. To cherish is to treasure. Oh, to treasure your wife. When she knows that you treasure her as a person, she is awakened from the inside out. You treasure her opinion, her intellect, her interests, and her sensitivity. You support her, care for her, look after her, and comfort her. This is cherishing her.

In doing so, you will be giving her the freedom to be more than the woman you dreamed about. She will reach new heights of expressing and experiencing things she didn't realize were possible. She will be free to become the woman God created.

Now, how is this done? First you must know that this love is what she needs. She needs love. She doesn't want it, she needs it. Know this deep in your being. Did I say she needs love? Okay.

To Nourish and to Cherish

Ted C. says that he loves his wife by first caring for her. He defines his caring as "doing something that she loves, even if he doesn't." He further gives the example that a pile of junk in the garage doesn't bother him but it does bother his wife, so he cleans it up. Caring is doing, and doing is love expressed. Jesus didn't feel like going to the cross, but He went because He cared. Ted says, "Caring is the fuel of my love."

Being that caring is paramount, you must perform Treasure Tasks. Treasure Tasks are those little nothings that say to her that she is always on your mind. These are the things done that continue to speak your love for her, to her.

Treasure Tasks
- Say to her daily, "I Love You!" (Remember, she needs this).
- Write little notes and post them on the mirror. Place love notes in her shoes, glove box, purse, etc.

    Example: Write a note that says, "I love your legs in these shoes!" This will *kill!*

- Send flowers because it's Tuesday.
- Low on funds? Pick some flowers from the road and make your own bouquet out of them.
- Celebrate your half-year anniversary. This doesn't have to be big. A card or quiet dinner will work.
- Celebrate her on holidays that mean nothing to you.
- Leave a singing voice message. (This is especially fun if you really cannot sing!)
- Scream a voice message: "I MISS YOUUUUUUUUUU!"
- Kiss her good-bye and hello.

Next, you can get touchy without sex. These actions will speak volumes of the closeness you share with her and no other. This is also essential foreplay that will pay off later. For the non-touchy, non-affectionate man, just remember it's not for you. You are not doing any of this selfishly. Know that each and every task or deed is for the love and needs of your wife.

- Rub her feet with baby oil.
- Massage her calves with baby oil.

- Rub her back with baby oil. (Better get some baby oil!)
- Use the magic of the short shoulder and neck rub.
- Give her a full back massage.
- Pat her on the rear as she passes by you. (Now watch her smile!)
- Hold hands in public and private.
- Give her a tender kiss in public.

Lastly, be creative. Be sure to help her laugh with you often.

Ed G. says he awakens and looks for different ways to serve his wife and be a better husband. He finds that being more attentive and listening to her helps him to make love an action.

Ed also honors her. This means that when she's not around, his conduct is always reflective of honor and respect for her.

The last part of Ephesians 5:29 states, "just as the Lord the church." Nourish and cherish your wife just as the Lord does the Church. In all our actions, we are simply striving to reach the measure of Christ.

Pastor Cory Hughes states that "compassion, understanding, sacrifice, and communication are vital to marriage." He further states, "It's not about me; therefore, I'll eliminate any attitude and swag because this is not an overnight endeavor. I must learn to communicate on her level until we find a level that fits the both of us."

This all plays a large role in nourishing and cherishing your wife. She must see, feel, and know that you care.

> "We pray for and with our wives. Leading biblical discussions all week, not only on Sunday."
> —Larenzo Fowler

CHAPTER 15

The Big Payoff

BEFORE DAVID FOUGHT Goliath, he asked a question in 1 Samuel 17:26. The verse says, "And David spoke to the men that stood by him, saying, 'What shall be done to the man that killeth this Philistine, and taketh away the reproach from Israel?'"

In other words, what do I get after I kill this dude?

And just like David, our journey is not without reward. We are rewarded with the opportunity to honor a woman, the opportunity to cover a woman, and the opportunity to love a woman. We are rewarded with the joys of marriage which include companionship and oneness. We are rewarded with a relationship which most closely resembles the relationship which God has with the Church. Yes, we are rewarded.

The most telling reward is stated in Ephesians 5:27 which states, "That he might present it to himself a glorious church, not having spot, or wrinkle, or any such thing; but that it should be holy and without blemish."

The ultimate presentation of the bride is when God presents her to Himself. Clean, pressed, bright and shining, holy, without blemish.

Husbands are awarded the privilege of presenting their wives to themselves. It looks something like this:

I present to myself – my wife, saved, sanctified, and Holy Spirit-filled. Complete in spirit, soul, and body. Full of confidence, glamour, and grace. Educated in the things of God's Word, institutes of higher learning, and the laws of the street.

My Wife. Beautiful, elegant, and eloquent. Purposeful, peaceful, and pleasant. Soulmate, companion, and friend. Lover, partner, and confidante.

My Wife. Size four and fine. Size twenty-four and mine. Or any size in between. She's my wife and I'm glad about it.

I present to myself a glorious wife, without spot or wrinkle or pimple or bump. Whole and holy, without blemish or any such thing.

My bride! My wife! My reward!

Brothers, this can be done and you're the man who can do it!

Now love her as Christ loved the church.

About the Author

REGINALD HOLDER IS a native of Nashville, Tennessee. He has been a faithful member of Born Again Church for over twenty-five years. His service through the years has included Sunday School teacher, usher, Prison Ministry, Intercessory Prayer Team, and MIHI (Made In His Image) Men's Ministry where he serves currently as the director.

Reggie offers extensive experience as a leader of men, sales trainer, and team builder. He attended Louisiana State University and has extensive training and certification from the American Association of Christian Counselors. He also serves as a Character Coach for high school and college students through working with the Fellowship of Christian Athletes.

As MIHI director, his greatest joy is when he sees men grow. He fully believes that as the man goes, so goes the family, the community, the school, and the church; therefore, he desires to see men whole, vibrant, and operating in the authority given to them as citizens of the Kingdom of God.

He is married to Dr. Greta Manning Holder. They have three daughters and three grandchildren, for whom he says it is his pleasure to be their covering.

For speaking engagements or ordering books contact:
Reggie Holder: Rholder78@gmail.com.

Order Information

REDEMPTION
P R E S S

To order additional copies of this book, please visit
www.redemption-press.com.
Also available on Amazon.com and BarnesandNoble.com
or by calling toll-free 1-844-2REDEEM.

CPSIA information can be obtained
at www.ICGtesting.com
Printed in the USA
LVHW051246260319
611871LV00001B/1/P

9 781683 145608